# Emily's Rescue

## MORGAN HARRISON

Ordering Information:

Prime Seven Media
518 Landmann St.
Tomah City, WI 54660

Printed in the United States of America

# Table of Contents

For all the Rheumatoid and Fibromyalgia
Suffers in the world.
Be strong and you will feel strong.

This story, short as it may be, could happen to men and women alike. If things had become as senseless and too much to cope with we become a Fibromyalgia Warrior as long as we fight it.

# Emily

I lived on the mainland of the Orkney Islands, at the top of Scotland. It is full of History and wonder. It was freezing in the winter, spring and Autumn, a bit warmer in the summer.

Today though, I stood at the Port of Stromness, which was home to the ferry that took you to Scotland itself. The port was deserted all most, except for the Ferry Captain and the few cars awaiting to board. It was early in the morning, and no one can see me wanting to escape.

'Why? am I here,' I said quietly to myself.

**'What are you doing?'** His voice from behind me in my ear.

I Jump and freeze as my heart beats like a freight train. 'Oh God, he is here,' I say.

But as I look, empty space, just my imagination. I sigh and relax. Then the memory of the slap that hurt because once before I tried to run away. Wincing at the invisible blow.

*'The day of the rest of my life, Emily Dawood is going to make it.'* I thought deep within my soul. *'The home of abuse and coldness has ended, and I Emily Dawood will prevail and get a better life,'* I yelled inside my head. *'My medical issues will burden him no more, Rheumatoid Arthritis and Fibromyalgia and all your problems associated with it will perish in a new world,'* I yell further. *'But, why do I feel so sick, nervous, and anxious,'* I ask myself.

My mood goes to hopeless again, because I am wasting away, and feel the smacks, punches, the kicks, and the verbal abuse surround me in darkness again, but it still must stop.

*'It was not my fault; it is not as if I wanted Arthritis and Fibromyalgia at the same time. The pain was all over my body, good and bad days. With my body tissues breaking down causing multiple skin and inside deterioration, I tried to be the best, but I can't do it, I can't take much more pain you hurt me with.'* I cry inside.

Look at me thin and pale, with a strong presence of frailness, my hair was not neat and shining, but scruffy and sad looking, like my eyes.

It was cold so I wrapped my coat around myself to try and protect the pain. My hair blew in the wind that came from the sea, the mousy brown but greying scruffy hair that looked like a bird's nest as it blew, tried to reach for the sky.

A flash back, as a boot launched itself into my face from above, seeing the angry hateful face of Dale standing over me, *'Just die already,'* he yelled at me.

I shivered and swayed a little, feeling nauseous. 'Gather yourself Emily,' I said aloud.

Looking up into the sky above there was some angry clouds whirling around in the vastness of the sky. The sea was choppy and not at ease today as the waves rose and crashed into the air, a storm was coming in.

*'Maybe it is angry at me for leaving so suddenly, running away, running for my life, away from the man I once loved that I thought loved me back,'* I thought *'Questions? Why has this happened to me? How could I have let it? I don't know how, changes were stressing for us, and thought he would get better,'* I added trying to justify why I stood here.

Now I am glued to the spot, fear from the wrath if caught, could someone have noticed and gone to tell him I am here?

'Oh gosh, please, no,' I said aloud.

The wind blew again, bringing my thoughts back down to earth and the here and now at this crucial place. I drew my coat tighter and not knowing what to do.

'Oh, why? Am I doing this?' I questioned aloud to the sea.

Emily's eyes shone blue and green in the rays of sunlight that peeked through the clouds that tried to light a spark but failed as her eyes dulled over again. Pain wracked her body, the body that wanted Scotland and freedom.

I wore Jeans that hung off me, that covered stick legs beneath, a blue shirt that covered me like a blanket and a blue cable knit jumper, black ankle boots very worn. I was anxious, painful as I stood glued to this spot for a while now. My back and hips were at the point of excruciating pain, shivering on flash backs of boots jamming hard into my back.

'*Hurry up Emily*,' I said to myself, looking around for prying eyes and ears.

Then I noticed the Ferry letting foot passengers on.

'Damn, you go, and never return, damn you Emily just go.' I yell

But glued to the spot I was, scared, dread washed over me and the hopelessness feeling that was bursting from my chest, as I could not breath.

Memories flashed before me, the scene that led to my Escape. The night was clearly a memorable one, the dinner that I cooked was cold now sitting on the table waiting for the wrath.

He came home with her in tow drunk as usual, laughing and jeering and ready to pour out the usual insults with the cracking sneer she wore.

She was a tall woman but thin always had her hair tied back, but quiet pretty compared to her stature with pretty eyes and a foul mouth. She always wore high heels and short skirts with a blouse to enhance her big breasts and they were big.

'Oh it's you,' she says with a burp.

Her face turned into a snarl as if I was dirt on the bottom of her shoe, then she would walk past me and push me to the floor. Laughing as she did so.

Dale was strong and still had his baby face that wore a beard quiet well with his wavey hair. He stood about five foot ten and still stayed gorgeous after all this time. How did he end up being a monster, the drinking, was it all because he had to run the farm when he wanted something more.

I thought maybe it is not his fault, but of course I was deluding myself because he was not a nice man after all, I knew he wanted to follow his own path, but he promised his mother he would take on the farm if needed. Giving up my dream to follow him into the unknown against my better judgement, but I did it anyway.

The years were rewarding I became a farmer and loved it. Milking the cows mucking out the sheds. But stopped when first my back went the joint swelling and the pain. A spinal fusion that took almost a year to get better, then Rheumatoid Arthritis and the Fibromyalgia set in, and the drugs made me scatty. Forget things, lose the words when talking, the tissue in the body would disintegrate before my eyes. The drugs would make me almost useless; this was something he couldn't cope with and the only way was to hurt.

Which lead to my mental state snapping, he hurt me and then it happened so fast. Grabbing the knife and quickly swung it with all my might at him, he dodges grabs my arm and turns the knife back towards me and penetrates my body instead. The pain of that pointed edge was like a pushing sensation with in my insides then blood.

That was it, that morning would be die or fly…

# Ben

Ben Hardy walked onto the Ferry with his large suitcase and big green duffle bag. He was handsome with his jet-black greying hair in a style that is becoming to his age, at fifty-seven years old and single. But the hareem of ladies back on the Island grew day by day. He has not bothered with another woman since his wife died thirty one years ago.

He was well built, muscular under his warm woolly clothes, wearing blue jeans and a cable knit white jumper and a black puffa coat. He threw his bag down on a spare seat on the outside of the ferry. Taking a seat next to his green duffle bag.

He stared at Fred the Captain of the Ferry as he worked on the ropes. Then his gaze wandered around the early morning movement on the port side and laid his eyes on a woman standing next to a car with a small overnight bag in her hands, that were shaking violently. She was glued to the spot and cold. He thought he had seen her once before with a broken leg about eight years ago.

'Hey Fred,' Ben shouted and getting up from his chair to move closer to Fred to talk.

Fred the Ferry Captain was hauling about the ropes. Dressed just like a ferry captain, with deep brown cord trousers that were old and baggy, rolled up at the bottom with calf length black almost wellies, and a dirty white cable knit jumper under a woollen brown jacket and a white and black skipper hat. His features were wind swept and had a seen a lot of sunshine and rain as his skin was a dirty brown colour with impaled wrinkles all over.

'Are you off yet?' Ben asked

'No, why? He replied stopping his rope gathering.

'That lady up there, she wants to come on the ferry,' Ben replied as he gazed up at the woman, who was still frozen to the spot.

'Miss Dawood, well I'll be,' Fred said surprised as he followed Bens pointing hand. 'God that poor woman,' was all he could say.

Ben was confused as to why he would say that 'Meaning what.' he said swallowing hard.

'Rumour has it, her fella Dale McDonald, beats her so bad she sleeps where she falls, and she is quiet poorly with Rheumatoid Arthritis and a thing called Fibromyalgia, her pain must be hell,' Fred bellowed out.

'Miss Dawood, well I'll be,' Ben began surprised 'That poor woman I have seen her once I think years ago when I first came here, sending her to see a specialist, God that poor woman.'

Ben felt the shame of men and women that beat on their spouses, Love is for ever not when it stops being normal and becomes defective. He was on the island for ten years as the doctor and had seen her on his files. He had sent her that first time to the Rheumatoid Department of the Hospital, I never even thought or even noticed, Domestic abuse from her other half, the one that is supposed to protect.

This was going to be bigger than he would have wanted, but she must get on board, to save Emily Dawood. He had to think quick, what shall I do?

'I am going to have a chat with her, is that ok Fred,' Ben asks.

Ben stood on his feet ready.

'Yep, thirty minutes and I must sail,' Fred replied 'Please bring her on board, just to save her,' He added sadly.

Ben left the Ferry and walked towards Emily Dawood, that he noticed was still frozen to the spot.

I barely registered the man talking to me, I came slowly down into myself in the frozen spot and felt the cold race through my body as I pulled my coat tighter and shivered.

'Miss Dawood,' His soft voice echoed around me.

'I am sorry,' I say in a worried voice.

Then I caught his beautiful brown hazel eyes looking back at me calm and inviting.

'Miss Dawood, do you want to get on the ferry?' he asked me as he meet my green and blue vacant eyes that showed such pain.

The life force was draining from my body. I was hurting badly, every bone was in agony, every muscle taught, moving seemed to hurt, but the ferry was my goal. The left side of my abdomen told me that I had to get on that ferry. Back home to my parents and safe.

*'Why, am I glued to the floor? I want to leave that monster,'* I cried almost aloud.

His eyes drew mine into his void of screaming at me 'I want to help you,'

'Is that your car,' Ben asked

'My partners car, yes,' Emily replied.

'Ditch it here, and let me take you home, or, even where you need to go, I have a car waiting at the other end,' Ben's voice hurried.

I locked with his eyes again and thought for a moment.

*'Ditching the car is a good Idea but going in the car with another man I just met seems odd,'* I thought. It put me off a little bit.

'I have little money,' I said wincing in pain and shivering. I locked eyes again with his.

'Wow, why am I getting butterflies,' Ben thought to himself, it made him feel odd. 'how old am I, not a teenager that is for sure, and the poor woman does not want a lurching man looking at her,' he added.

'I will pay for all the expenses, including food, drink, and petrol, there is no worries there,' He blurted out.

I was taken aback by his kindness; he was handsome and seemed to be gentle in his mannerisms and ways. His age was like me in his fifties, he wore a tired face with his hair greying, he has seen a lot of life, people like me.

*I possess an overnight bag and that is it, everything else was left as this was a quick escape, was I kidding. Being passed from one man to the other. I don't care now if I am free away from that.*

'Does that mean Yes? He asked.

'You are not a serial killer, are you?' I asked, as I melted in his chocolate eyes.

*'Chocolate, what? What am I thinking,' I thought 'Not that it made any difference. I wanted off the Island, because, if not, I would have killed myself, I could not endure any more, but snapping in the end turned out on his favour again and left me with a lot of no hope.*

'She looks as white as a sheet and very frail to the touch, her figure is half starved and bony. No one really knows her pain and secrets, but her,' Ben thought as he watched her.

'Here let me take your bag,' he offered, then he offered his hand.

I was touched and worried. My hand moved to take his, I gasp and pull away, shook my head, and took his hand. His hand was soft and clean of hard labour. My hand was engulfed in his, it left me speechless and flustered.

Sparks and a warm feeling came over Ben 'What is this feeling,' he thought 'She makes me feel alive again after all these years of numbness, no can't be,' her hand was so soft and cold very thin and bony.

I was warmed by his touch, how cool it made me feel, restful and safe. *'But what is this?'* tummy with butterflies, my heart is beating so fast out of my chest. How old am I, not a teenager that is for sure. Men no more,' I thought with happy and sad thoughts.

This handsome Knight that took my hand and led me to the edge of the Island.

But taking those steps to the Ferry, raked me in awful pain, every step was terrible, the glue was giving way, the big dressing will hold a little while. But I was going, leaving my days on the Island that was far too long, longer than they should have been. But precious days to come in the form of freedom.

'Thank you,' I say smiling to anyone that may have heard.

He smiled and guided Miss Emily Dawood to the ferry, with those last few steps to never return.

I smiled with the feelings inside of pure relief and pending loneliness.

# Ferry

en took me onto the Ferry and into the lounge area, it was under cover so not cold. The Ferry had two lorries and four cars that sat below huddled together until time to get off.

The Lounge was cosy with a few windows for staring out to sea when the ferry crosses the open seas. I could see the choppy sea and the storm clouds above, they mostly hung over the Island, so it gave us safe passage out of the bay. The seats in the lounge were comfortable with patterned red and green seat covers like a bench all the way around. Table and chairs, to compliment the seating areas. A few vending machines to get a drink from, be all right if I had any money on me, then in the middle was a small shop that sold sandwiches, drinks, and sweets.

I sat at a window seat at an angle for me to see the Port and who was coming for me. Ben had gone back outside to collect his bags and bought them back in and laid them on the floor.

The pain came back vigorously, the hole in my left side was glued together the strongest glue I could find. The dressing was there to keep it clean and free from bacteria getting in, although it was making me feel sick and dizzy at times. My head began to ache, and my tummy rumbled loudly for my hunger grew wild within me.

'So where are you wanting to go, when we get to the mainland,' Ben questioned 'Because if I am taking you, I would need to know.' He says finding the conversation for her to open up.

'A Village called Dawood not far from Axminster,' I say 'Do you know it,' I asked.

Ben sat up and was speechless a few moments.

'Axminster, what a co-incidence, I am off to Axminster, which is where I am going to work and live. Love the hospital there,' he really was taken aback on the co-incidence.

'That is good fortune for me then,' I smiled a bit weary of the way he bubbles.

'I hope you will be safe and warm,' He replies softly.

I fell silent as the ferry began to feel the waves as we left the Island behind. *'Free, Free,'* I thought.

Then suddenly, the emotion of this freedom began to cloud all my senses and judgement and I began to cry and could not stop the tears.

Ben's heart was leaping with over whelming pity for her.

**'She does not need pity, she needs comfort,'** He thought.

Ben moved closer to me, and slowly began to take my hand, by touching my fingers.

'What is this feeling, electricity jolt sunk into every vein that it could, followed by those annoying butterflies in the tummy, how old am I,' Ben Thought suddenly smiling.

I felt something, and quickly pulled away my hand, '*What is this feeling, he felt warm, safe, and inviting. This touch has made my body feel human once more,*' I thought smiling at him slightly.

'Let me take your hand, please, don't cry, at least let me issue some comfort. It is over now, time for a new chapter in your life, a new you,' Ben says but not so sure about pity but the way he felt about her was to care and support.

I let him softly take my hand in his, it felt warm and soft and, What the Hell? Tummy doing leaps and bounds.

Ben gave me a pack of travel tissues to dry my eyes as he kept hold of my hand. It was not a problem, and I did not mind, because he felt safe, which was something I have not felt in a long time, or what seemed like for ever.

'You travel light,' he says nodding at my bag 'Is that an overnight bag?' he asked softly.

'Yes,' I say 'these are the only things I own in the world, having the clothes on my back as the only outfit and what is in the bag,' I winced in pain and felt my face drain of any colour.

I came over all hot, cold, and dizzy, could feel myself swaying a little and the sick feeling like a wave through me. '*I hope I will not be sick here, must keep it together,' I thought.*

'Are you ok, you're looking a bit green,' Ben began concerned. He was still holding my hand.

*'Can I really feel something after all these years of numbness, I promised, no more,'* I thought.

'Can I really feel something after all these years, I promised no one will ever compare,' Ben tangled with his thoughts. 'Oh Cassie!'

Ben sat watching how I moved and how I must be feeling, holding my hand, to him, felt bony and cold, the gnarled fingers that is wracked with Rheumatoid Arthritis, and dry skin on the bones beneath. So delicate yet soft and small. His heart pinged as if a jolt of lightening hit it, and sparks jolted through his body. A wave of warmth and energy sprang through his body, looking deep into her eyes he sees the pain and decided was this pity he was feeling. For the life she thought she was going to have with the man she thought that loved her, instead she has endured a life of hate and abuse, she became unattractive to him through illness. He could only imagine the trauma she has lived through, now with her broken body mousy brown hair with greying parts that fell across her gaunt white face and shoulders, to the blemishes of red blotches on her peaky face. No make-up just pure her, What? He suddenly thought bringing himself back to the now, shaking his head. He promised his late wife forever and a day. The only love of his life.

'But, why? Do I feel something that has been dead for a long time,' He asks himself with strange butterflies.

'You look a bit under the weather, are you ok?' he asks concerned, still holding my hand.

'I feel unwell, but need to go home far away from there,' I cried 'Promise me you will get me home dead or alive,' I say panicked and putting my hand over his other hand.

Ben sat shocked at the words Dead or Alive, they struck a panic jolt within him. 'Ok,' he replies.

'Where are you running to? Ben questioned.

'My parents live in the village of Dawood; they live in the Manor House there. I want to see them, but I don't know if they will have me back after all these years,' I said putting my face to the floor in shame.

'What are you running from? He asked but was cautious.

Pain crashed through my body at the thought of all those memories like a freight train crashing through the station. I wanted to keep it supressed as every thrashing from him came rushing back. The man that loved me once.

'He changed because I changed. It was my fault that it happened, I was useless and broken. I cry, I have not cried in many years, they seemed to have dried up, yet here I am,' I cried, as I shook and trembled. 'I forever will feel those punches and kicks, the insults, the belittling, and the loveless hole within me will never leave,' I add looking back at the floor and back to his eyes.

Ben could see the hurt and pain in her eyes, which engraved into his soul forever. That was when he looked away in shame.

'Ben, please don't pity me,' I asked. 'I let this happen.'

Ben looked back into her eyes, 'Somehow, you know that what you have endured is hard for those that have not felt that pain, we cannot find the correct words to say, I am lost, we are lost,' Ben says making eye contact with me.

'I am so sorry, I make you feel that way, you see if I did not escape today. You know get on the ferry, I would have gone home and killed myself. Does that explain the pain better,' I say looking back into his eyes.

Ben's heart cracked and shattered into a million pieces and his body slumped forward, 'Now I want to take you in my arms and hold up. But….,' he began 'Well you are here on the ferry, and I will get you home.' he sheds a tear.

I smiled a grateful smile at him. 'So what are you running away from Ben hardy,' I asked

He looked at me, and sadness mellowed his mood, and he took a few moments to collect himself.

'My Wife,' he says looking at me with a great deal of sadness.

'Sorry I asked that question,'

Ben said no more on the subject.

'How far do you think we are away from the mainland,' I asked breaking the sombre mood. It was a sad moment we shared, but reality is where we need to be. I could not see either place just water.

Outside was grey and dark as if we were leaving the storm behind us and followed ever so slowly, but the rain did slash the windows.

'Free,' I say aloud. My heart was thumping as if telling me this is too good to be true.

'Are you hungry,' Ben asked 'I will get some snacks and drinks from the kiosk.' He stood to leave.

I grabbed his hand with my white cold bony hand, it screamed warmth.

'Emily, are you ok?' He asked me concerned.

I sat and he stood, Ben felt a jolt of passion in her hold, he held her hand carefully, as he thought, as delicate as a flower, then be bent down. 'Emily,' he began

'Thank you so much, thank you,' I say beginning to cry.

Ben down on one knee, hugged me carefully, I winced in pain, but it was worth it. His gentle nature and heart felt touches and feelings made me feel alive.

'Sorry, snacks,' He says pulling away as if he had done something wrong.

He was so safe, to feel and to hold. His delicate manner pulled at my heart.

'You ok now?' He asked. 'I promise to come back,'

'Yes,' I replied drying my eyes.

'Ok, I will be back in a minute,' he left for the kiosk.

My smile turned into agony in my face 'Please stay closed,' I whispered to myself. The pain jingled through my body like hot poker rods. I shook in pain trying to keep myself together and sitting up.

Ben was gone for a few minutes, and then came back carrying drinks, sandwiches, and crisps.

'Sorry they did not have much,' he said putting them on the table. 'Is it ok if I sit closer to you, as I noticed earlier you were shivering and maybe body heat could warm you up,' he began 'Nothing in it of course,' he flustered.

I smiled as much as I could and then nodded to say ok then.

He did, he moved close and touched my body so lightly. It was wonderful the light tingles of energy that ran through my body like heeling hands. Those feelings are what I so craved for a long time.

'The food, is there some for me?' I asked stomach rumbling.

'Yes, have whatever you like,' He said taken aback by the question.

'You mean I can have a whole sandwich, and some crisps and a hot tea,' I said shocked, 'food for me'

The hot tea warmed my hands and my heart, the food was great, and I was grateful for the kindness.

> I am Emotionally damaged, manipulated
> in so many ways, then you came
> and made me feel whole, but you were
> emotionally damaged, as his wife died
> tragically young, we can fix ourselves.

# Breakfast

The morning went on with Orkney moving further and further away, my desperate moments were fading into freedom. Is he there oblivious to my escape, the pain stabbed me again, the mental pain of being told 'You are a bad person, and what happens to bad people,' He would say and smile like a man possessed, as he passed out the punishment.

'Miss Dawood, do you have any medication?' ben asked quietly 'you seem to be in a lot of pain, Rheumatoid Arthritis and Fibromyalgia is not an easy thing to cope with,' He added

I was in my own thoughts when his voice broke through the memory of punishment. 'No, what sort of medication?' I ask

'Anything that helps with the disease, swelling, erm, Methotrexate, pregabalin and injections, blood pressure tablets, anything at all?' Ben asked.

'Nothing, they were taken from me by my husband and never gave me them.' I say remembering the pain and no drugs to heal.

Tears began to escape from nowhere, 'Not sure if they are happy or sad tears, I'm sorry,' I apologize.

'Miss Dawood, I am sorry to make you remember,' Ben says brushing my hair from my face.

'Please call me Emily,' I say crying.

'Emily what is the matter?' Ben asks not knowing what to do.

'Sorry, I got away, but to go where, will my mum and dad still want me after all this time. My children I need to face them and tell them that I Love them so much and how sorry I am. If I make it there.' I cried uncontrollable; this made my side hurt.

'Emily, I understand to a degree, I can't begin to calculate all the extras when one is trapped and suddenly set free from the cage when the door is ajar. To run and never look back, only forward and to have paths to choose. But let us get through the journey stage by stage, and I can help you, and perhaps you can help me,' Ben said with my hand in his and staring into my eyes. 'The hardest part of living is fighting our darkest demons,' he adds smiling

My tears stopped flowing as I intently listened to his soft sincere voice, both of us had demons to air out and fight against.

'I would like to sleep safely in a bed and wake up in the sunlight and be able to feel good about myself,' I say 'But, you want to help with these simple requests,' I added shocked staring into his tearful eyes.

I push my body closer to him for the body heat.

Ben's phone rang in his jacket pocket, he raised his eyebrows, and pulled it out, then swiped the green button to answer it.

'John, what is it?' he asks. Silence as John spoke on the other end as it ticked by his shoulders slumped 'Oh, about eleven o'clock, ok, we will wait,' he adds 'thank you,' he puts the phone back in his pocket.

'Bad news,' I ask panicking.

'Just the car, needed an overhaul, so that it is road worthy, it will be by at around elevenish. Not too bad, time for a healthy meal, breakfast,' He replied smiling.

'Ok,' I became nervous.

I really did not want to wait around here, too close to the port.

'Emily we will be safe, and we will be on our way soon, I promise,' Ben smiled putting his hand over mine to calm me.

Finally, the Ferry was piloted into the port of Scrabster the top end of Scotland.

Ben pulled all his bags together and Emily pulled hers closer.

'Welcome to the United Kingdom and your freedom, your chauffeur is hungry. So, let us have breakfast,' he chirped.

I was quiet, as I watched Ben Hardy, his ways, and his mannerisms. His features were warm, but also ageing gracefully. The way his eyebrows raised up when he thought he said the wrong thing. His hands were soft as they were caring and warm.

Ben watched Emily and found that her pale face was radiating sadness and held a lot of pain and history. Her smile was alluring, and her body was soft to the touch and weak, he wanted to put her in his pocket and keep her safe.

The ferry began to let off the vehicles and then the foot passengers began to disembark onto the land.

I walked off with Ben, had to walk slower because my body hurt and was afraid the wound would open. It made me feel nauseated that came over me like a wave.

Being away from the atmosphere of that place, the air felt fresh and calm. '*Thankyou Ben Hardy for dragging me on to that ferry and thank you for caring for me,*' I thought as I stared at the back of his head.

He was strong as he carried his heavy bags, his black hair greying with a stray strand of hair flapping in the wind.

'Welcome to Scotland Emily Dawood, freedom awaits you,' he said with happiness and joy for me.

I could not smile, like I should do. But inside I am bursting with happiness and joy but smiling on the outside was far away.

'Freedom, but still to close,' I whispered aloud.

'Ok, car not yet ready, so over there is a café and the best breakfast in the world,' Ben smiled.

Ben entered the Café with all his bags, I followed behind cautiously. He chose a table by the window and put his bags on the opposite seats and sat next to Emily on the brown cushioned seat as he wanted her to feel safe and warm.

'Good morning, Ben how are you these days?' the waitress questions as she came walking towards us.

She was about sixty something and her face was wrinkled and her skin was like chicken skin, you know when you have plucked the feathers off. Brown greying hair and wore a bubbly body and even bubblier smile for Ben.

'Good Morning, lovely, could we have two breakfasts and a coffee and a strong tea, please,' Ben said smiling 'You know Bev I am good, and yourself?'

'Who is this young lady?' Bev questioned raising an eyebrow.

'Oh sorry, this Emily, we are travelling together and even going to the same place,' Ben said pointing to me.

'Hello, Emily,' Bev said with a big smile.

I felt sick at this stage, I could feel all the colour drain from my body, the pain from my stab wound was making my stomach burn hence the sick feeling.

'Are you all right Miss,' Bev asked concerned.

'Yes, sorry, just a little nausea,' I replied holding my tummy.

Bev walked off to get our drinks and breakfast, her hips wriggling with her weight.

'Gosh I'm starving,' Ben says putting his hands on his tummy, grabbing, and then patting it.

'You must be a regular if she knows you so well,' I say to him.

Ben bent his head and shoulders deflated and heavy hearted.

'Ben, what are you really running from?' I asked him sadly.

I looked deep into his eyes as he turned his head away, then turned again to look at me his eyes full of sorrow. With hurt and overwhelming sadness.

There were a few moments of silence.

'If I tell you, will you tell me your story?' He asks softly, looking down and back into her eyes.

In my eyes, he saw hell, pain and despair and they screamed at him for help, to hold me to love me and to save me. To make me feel better, to help, but how can he help me. I thought for a few moments.

'Deal, you go first,' I say.

The breakfast and the drinks arrived. The plates were massive, bacon, eggs, sausage, beans, mushroom, croquets, and sourdough bread.

'Ben,' I asked

'Yes,' he replied

'Is this food really all for me, I mean all of it to eat?' I asked taken aback.

'Yes love, it is all for you, enjoy,' Bev smiled and walked away. Setting the condiments on the table.

'Wow, all for me,' I almost cried.

We both tucked into the hearty breakfast, I ate slow as not to be sick, but it was wonderful, and I began to cry as I ate it. It was uncontrollable and it made me so happy.

'Is that good?' Ben asked.

'Fab,' I cried eating.

I looked into his heavy eyes, 'You don't have to tell me anything, no pressure,' he says.

Ben went back into his own thoughts.

'I still wear my wedding ring after so long,' he began touching his wedding ring 'We met in college and then went to the same university. Graduated after five years and married at twenty-two, she was twenty-three. We had a boy, beautiful boy. Named him Casey, but he is thirty-two now and an amazing doctor. I gained him and lost her at the same time. Could not save her, all the doctors and nurses could not control her bleeding, and bled to death there and then,' he hung his head as he flashed back to that moment. 'But, she told me in that moment, never give up and keep our promise, to the fact you can and find love again, then she died.'

I stopped eating and looked horrified then sorrow, I stared at him with pity and heartache, all that I could give him. I put my head on his arm and my hand on his.

Ben gasped and his heart thumped, tears formed in his eyes.

'We named him Casey because her name was Cassie. He has moments when he feels he is to blame for her death. That pain of those feelings sometimes kills him inside, and I cannot dowse that fire within him,' Ben added.

'Ben, stop, please,' I cried in more tears 'Your pain is killing me, it is too heavy, and I am too weak to carry it for you,'

'Oh no don't cry Emily please,' Ben begged worried.

My wound was hurting, and I felt it unsealing. I had to try and make myself stop crying.

'Ben, these tears are for your sadness, if you can't cry. My diseases have stopped me from crying for myself, these tears are flowing out, the tears for you, because I feel for you Ben.' I cried.

'Do you know you have these diseases, by a doctor,' Ben asks.

'Yes Rheumatoid Arthritis and Fibromyalgia, was not expecting what comes with it, with the cruelty on top,' I reply.

'I am sorry,' He says lowering his head

'Have you ever been loved, and have you ever loved someone over the years. Did they love you for pity's sake,' I asked cautiously.

'No, my body and heart and mind tell me no, been alone all these years. You know I did, you looked so pitiful standing there, yes, and that was then, but now you are,

We went silent for a few moments.

'It began at college, and we were eighteen, he was my boyfriend and played in a band. He wanted to go to university to study Criminal Psychology, but, one day a call came, his dad has passed away. That he was needed back to the farm in Orkney,' I began, I took a drink of tea.

'He said he had to give up his dream and being his girlfriend at that time tried to console him. But he lashed and broke my arm and gave me a black eye. You would have thought then something was wrong, my mum and dad could see it, but I went with him to the farm anyway. Worst decision I have ever made, he was changing but I loved him. We had two children, a boy, and a girl,' I stopped and fell silent, those words were hard to keep going, 'B-both, through him forcing himself on me whilst drunk, I love them to death anyway.

I fell silent and sat motionless for a few moments, then drank some more tea.

Ben lost his appetite 'I'm sorry,' is all he could say.

We both went back to sort of eating in silence that became deafening.

Luckily, Ben's car turned up. After breakfast I had to visit the bathroom, whilst Ben packed his bags into his blue as deep as the ocean Range Rover. I uncovered my wound in the mirror, 'Stayed glued, but still bleeding, my skin was looking an odd colour of black and sticky red. The pain enshrouded me as I put on a new dressing from my bag and discarded the old one in the bin.

'Don't think about it,' I tell myself aloud.

Outside Ben had packed his bags away and was ready to go. His smile radiated through me and made it all worthwhile. I looked away ashamed.

'Have you never left the Island, until now,' He asked his voice sad.

The road ahead is busy and long, *'Can I really make it, will he make that happen?'* I asked myself.

'No, I hardly stepped out of the house, I want to see the stars in the sky on the beach with him, but he changed so much. Most days I could not move, because he hurt me so bad, why? Would he do that. I wanted to see the stars shooting across the sky. The sun burning my skin as I walked the cliffs and the fields. Just be me, stop the pain, but the doctors say this is my life, and no one will ever love me again or even touch me,' I answered with despair and heartache.

Ben stepped forward and held me so softly and with care.

'You know we can do that,' Ben began 'See the stars, so what do you say we go,'

We were on the road at last leaving the ferry port behind us, far behind us.

'You have the entire world ahead of you now.' He smiled 'So good morning, young lady, my name is Ben Hardy am I am a widower,' He said introducing himself.

'Good Morning, Ben, my name is Emily Dawood, and I have been Rescued and now free, so damn free,' I smiled happily.

I felt inside the elation of power of freedom and the power to choose to go anywhere. *'Could I really wear what I wanted and have a crush on someone close,'* I say inside, I smiled.

'Yes, you are free and that means you can choose your own clothes, choose your own path, what you want,' Ben said unexpected as if he could read my mind.

'Do you think my children will see me, and any grandchildren they may have,' I say aloud and smile, but I know that stage is far off.

'You know Emily, I am so pleased to meet you,' Ben said stealing a glance at me taking his eyes off the road, then back again.

'Yes, I you Ben,' I smiled back

I sat in silence thinking about my children and how have they grown up, my mum and dad would have seen to that. But they may not want to see me, I would understand if they thought better to stay away. It was all my fault, spending just twelve years of their lives with them until my mum and dad took them away, they would keep them safe from him. I could not take any more abuse from him for them, he would stoop so low as to strike his own children. They would cry a long time for me, and it made them scared, who could live like that. But they are safe. I smiled.

'Penny for those thoughts,' Ben said breaking through my wall.

> My Body is a temple of energy, but only ancient, crumbling, cursed and haunted by memories.

# Moving On

I suddenly felt a pang of guilt.

'You don't have to take me you know, I can find public transport,' I say 'I feel guilty you must do this, you are such a sweet, nice man,'

'This is my pleasure to take a lady home, beside what sort of man would I be if I dragged you here and left you alone,' Ben replied smiling.

'Funny those days are now, a distant memory. Oh, to be young again, we could change a few things,' I said quietly.

*'This man, this handsome fit professional man, took my hand at the ferry port because I was glued scared and timid. He came with his kind words and warm angel eyes and helped me. The thing is why? He could have left me there, why? Was he blessed with helping me. I am not beautiful, no makeup, scruffy hair that has lost its way. Hunched*

*with pain to a point, what? Must he think of me, it is like something from a romance novel, the perfect man that saves the damsel. Being weak and feeble I thought a man would run a mile, are they not all the same, just shout and hit you, say sorry and build you up for the next one. But no, they are not, there are some Princes out there,'* I thought as I looked at him and his soft features and smile.

'I have snacks and a couple of books for the journey, Romance Novels most ladies like those.' He says holding up a plastic bag with items in.

I took it and fished through it, Ali McNamara – Secrets and Seashells at Rainbow Bay and Debbie Macomber – Dashing Through the Snow, they both looked good.

'Thank you,' I replied.

'Do you think you could chat with me a little as I drive,' He asked.

I nodded yes. Suddenly pain racked my body, the wound was burning my insides and I felt a little sick.

'The year 2008 changed my life, well 1986 to be exact. 2008 my back was damaged, and I had a spinal fusion on L4 and L5 vertebrae, it took six months to get better. I suppose that is when he lost it for good, because it was difficult to have sex and he was mad, he would hit me for being useless and weak, his demeaner towards me got more of a hatred stare. It all had to end, it for me at the time was kill or be killed but I lost that fight, so it was run and get off this land and run,' I said looking at the floor. Holding my side.

'Emily stop if it hurts you,' Ben pleaded.

I went quite a while.

'Do you need to make a stop anywhere?' He asked me.

'Erm, Lochness, can we go, I would like to see the beauty, the ladies told me how amazing it was with the stars over the lake in the dark, I have not left the Island for twenty years,' I cry but keep my composure.

'What? Did you say,' he snaps with shock. 'You have never left for twenty years,'

'Yes, I was just remembering stuff,' I say and sort of smiled.

'Can I ask a question in a roundabout way?' He asks looking at . me quickly and then back to the road.

'Yes,' I reply

'Are you in a great deal of pain?' His asks as his eyebrows scrunch lightly together anticipating the answer. 'You know with things,' he added.

I thought a few moments, '*What to say? How much to say? Does he know?*'

'I am yes, but talk about that when I can, I want to enjoy the time we have,' I reply sadly.

'Ok, I know you will tell me,' he replies smiling a sad smile.

He smiled and watched the road ahead. 'What is going on?' he asked himself 'Why do I feel like a teenager with all the motions of puppy love. Is that what it is? Love? I don't know anything about her, what she has been through, how her mental state is. Then, can she love another man so soon, but could this just be pity for the situation and for her, may well be? But I have feelings of love that cause my heart to race and flutter. She is trusting, gentle and fragile, hurting a lot, she may tell me why. I am a man and I have eyes that can see her agony.' He thought

'Penny for those thoughts Ben,' I say softly.

He turned to look at me quickly.

'I know,' he began as his eyes lit up as he turned back to the road.

'What?' I questioned.

'We are moving on, in the new life of Miss Emily Dawood,' Ben began 'Have you ever heard of Brora beach,' he asks.

'Sorry No,'

'We are having a stop and after that Dunrobin Castle, then the rest stop Lock Ness for the Stars, it is well worth a look,' He said squealing like a little kid.

I was quiet and taken aback by his outburst. 'That sounds good,' I say. Then silence.

'He did not want to look after the farm, but he had no choice. I loved him and to me and him that was all that mattered at the time. But he began to change, I would cook dinner, and he would come home, it started with not the dinner he wanted. He would throw the plate at me, and I would have cooked him what he wanted, then he would slap me, it made him feel better and always ended up with bruises that you could not see. I covered them up.' I said as I covered my face in shame.

Ben listened, that is what Emily needed, to be loved. He was sickened to the core. But he listened.

'But, overall, it took away all my years that I planned for myself. The fun times that families should have. Holidays, presents, cuddles all with the children,' I said quietly to myself, and began to sob quietly.

Ben's Heart was crushed, and he wanted to touch her and hold her.

'Oooohhh, look the sign for Brora Beach,' he smiled.

Silence fell, me with my demons and Ben with his heartache.

I sat and thought. 'I left my medication I left it at home, and everything hurts. My fingers swelled, I was so tired, headache and poorly skin. What is to become of me, from alive to almost dead. Dead everywhere and things that no man would want to touch.

# Brora Beach

B en turned onto the small road that was only a one car passing place, the road was no trouble as it was empty.

'Why did I pick her up and offer her to be my passenger? Why?' He thought. 'She is so very fragile, in a lot of pain and screaming for help. So did I … no she has had a lot to deal with, smiling at me even though she is tired with pain. For her this makes the world feel better somehow. But my pain that I hold inside is bursting to get out and talk to her about it. But I am a man, she may not listen to me. All those years the feelings tried to consume me, in ways that only I could possibly imagine. Alone scared for the future and what would lay ahead. Yep, I have tried to move on with a couple of ladies, but nothing came, no feelings, no thought, no love. Was I a bad person? That no one has measured up to my love,' He thought 'But, here I am like a love-struck teenager at fifty-seven, liking these feelings for a woman so plain and white, no make-up, no clothes, no nothing but mentally broken,' He added.

I was smiling to a degree.

'Was it pity?' he thought 'Or was it something within me that has changed. Yes, pity and yet love. Love the woman that is so scared of men because all she sees is violence and pain. But we all have our own personalities and how we react to a woman. I want to take her in my arms and hold her so gentle and pure,' He thought smiling.

Ben pulled into the car park for the beach and came to a halt in the parking bay.

'This is so beautiful,' I say.

'Emily?' Ben asked

'Yes,' I replied.

'Erm, do you not feel uneasy with me?' He asked as he fell over the steering wheel.

'In what way?' I ask

'Being a man and this road trip,' he adds.

'Well, I am nervous when you come near me. It frightens me. But even so, you feel kind and care for people. You may get angry but would never hurt another person or me, I may not be pretty, my hair is a terrible mess, I am white and thin. Not nice to look at,' I replied looking into his eyes and then the floor.

'You know you have beautiful eyes that catches a man's heart,' he said smiling.

He made me blush. 'Thank you,' I say

'You can talk to me if you need to, doctors do listen,' He said gently.

'You can talk to me if you need to,' I say back with a slight smile.

Silence fell again.

We got out of the vehicle, and I wrapped my coat tighter around me and held onto my left side, wincing in pain. Ben took his phone out and looked at it and then put it away. His face went white.

'Ben are you all right, you look a bit peaky,' I ask concerned.

'Sorry, yes fine,' he replied 'So don't you think this is beautiful,'

I turned my gaze to the white golden sands and blue sea. There was no one around, just us and the sands and water and sky.

Ben had opened the back of the Range Rover and pulled out two-fold out chairs and two towels. In his cooler that he had in the boot stocked with drinks, and a lunch box times two, with crisps.

'Wow, who packed all that up. Someone loves you,' Emily smiled.

'Bev, she is amazing, like a mum to me,' He said smiling. 'Now are you going to paddle in the sea, which is the reason for the towels. My female friend.' Ben began all excited.

We both sat and removed our shoes and socks.

'It is freezing,' I say.

'It is October,' Ben replies. 'Shall we walk,'

I looked at his soft brown eyes, and watched his hair blow slightly in the wind, and how the sun fell onto his face, lighting up all his wrinkles and showing his blemishes, it warmed my heart. His long eyelashes, sparkles of grey in between. The stubble on his face looked soft to the touch.

'Yes, let's walk,'

The sand under my feet felt so soft and it seemed that you sank in it. Ben grabbed my hand, which made me gasp, but he felt so caring, so I let him.

'Gosh, she is so thin and white,' Ben thought. He watched as a faint smile passed her lips that were such a white colour. 'They are so kissable, what? Am I saying, sorry love I promised,'

I was finding it difficult and tired walking on the sand, my wound screamed at me, and my body hurt. But it felt good, freedom and fresh air.

'Ben,' I say. We reached the water's edge and stopped.

'Yes,' He said putting his toes into the chilly water

'Erm…………,' I began and faltered. 'Thank you for saving me,' With tears in my eyes.

Ben gasped. 'Emily, glad that I did, I would not want you to come to any harm,' he replied.

Silence fell again as I put my foot into the sea, I gasped, 'It's so cold,' I say.

Ben laughed.

'My wife was everything to me. My boy Casey is a mental note to stay strong. I miss her every day and thought I could never love another woman. That was twenty-two years ago. Here I am today fifty-seven and still missing her,' Ben said as he watched beyond the ocean. Then his head to the ground.

I looked at the ocean horizon.

'Ben, you love her, and that kind of love is a gift to hold onto, but she also would not like the fact you never had a relationship and been lonely all this time. It is torture for you every day, and it should be peace and happiness you feel, she is always available to talk with you, she may not say a lot, but I know she would want you to be happy and smile again,' I say holding his hand tighter.

The sea water lapped over our feet and ticked our toes.

'But, you see, I cannot mourn forever Emily, life needs to go on,' He mourned.

'That is true, time does not need to stand still, but you will know when you will move on, it will be in your heart,' I say softly.

Silence once more, my pain was getting to the stinging stage. Ben stared at me in awe, then at the sand. He walked a little up the beach and picked up a shell. Then he washed it shaking it dry, then on his shirt under his jumper he wiped it dry. He then walked back and opened his hand with it in, the shell was a creamy colour, quite large with curly edges with a deep caramel colour.

'Here a gift for you and the first day of freedom, also the day you met me,' He says smiling.

I took the shell in my hand and was awed by how soft it feels, then held it with my right hand to my chest.

'Thank you, it's perfect,' I say smiling.

'She is so perfect,' Ben thought as he watched her holding it to her chest.

'He was the perfect husband, I was an ungrateful and difficult wife, he would tell me coldly. I began to see the stranger in his eyes and my world began to crumble away.' I just remembered that moment, can't relive those feelings again.

Ben listened, he stood close to her, close enough to kiss her. 'What?' stop that. He shook his head, but those thoughts would not leave him.

'I became his punching bag, and he hurt me so badly, crushed my spine, hence the spinal fusion. I was moulded into a state of submission, of fear and obedience. After that it started to become a blur, Arthritis and then followed by the Fibromyalgia. I was completely broken and alone,' I say remembering in a flash back. 'The truth is I can't, I can't do it anymore.'

Feeling a bit sick and weak I fell against the side of his body. I heard him gasp.

'Emily,' He said, on impulse he held her softly in his arms and planted a kiss on the side of cheek. 'You are not broken, just fragile and kind,' talking into her hair, 'it is lonely with no one to help, and have the feelings of pity and hurt, and harsh words and comments from those that are meant to protect you. It is not easy to forgive yourself which is the worst pity of all.'

I was enjoying his embrace all though I was shaking.

'Now shall we sit and enjoy a drink and crisps,' He asked taking my hand and leading me back.

'The beach is scenic and the perfect place to be when you need to chill and think,' I say. Struggling in the sand. My hand was still in his.

The ocean was calm today, and the waves were lapping at the sand, the small sand dunes had grass growing from them.

We sat on the chairs and Ben pulled out drinks and crisps.

'We have lunch elsewhere,' He said munching on cheese and onion crisps.

'Thank you for sharing with me,' I smile 'It makes me happy for my final few days,' I add.

She looked me in the eyes full of cloudiness. 'Final days, what? Do you mean,' He begged as he snapped the words out.

'For all this, and taking me home,' I say 'then we will be parting ways, and I may never see you again,' I add Playing it safe.

Ben sat and thought a while, 'Not sure what is going on?' he thought laying his eyes on her. Holding her hand was magical, my heart pumped, and he could feel twinges in areas he would not like public. I met a strange woman, and she is so nice and smiles at me, through all her pain and anguish. I like the closeness and she feels warm and kind, I want to keep her safe,' He adds.

My hair blew in the wind and across my face.

*'Ben is so thoughtful, he feels so natural, kind, and warm, I need him to feel safe and good about himself, before I die. Let's be honest with this festering hole in my side would make way to infection and death. But I want to be with him, him to take care of me make me feel safe. Thank you, Ben Hardy,'* I thought as I sat next to him.

Ben Packed away all his gear into the back of the vehicle, the next thing was to tackle the sand on our toes, it took ages to clean.

# The Stars

We got back on the road, back in the warmth of the vehicle.

There was silence for a while as we drove, my pain was getting to the point of crying, and the vehicle sometimes jolted my wound that I needed to stay closed.

'Do you like the stars,' Ben asks.

'Yes, I want to see a sky full of stars, at home I would see a few out of my window. Otherwise without a peek I just hid away.' I replied

'Excellent luckily, I know a good spot, and it will be a clear night as well,' Ben said excitedly.

'Really,' I said feeling alive once more.

'There is a bed and breakfast on Loch Ness that I know, I always stay there, and you will love Maggs who runs it, she is lovely,'

'That sounds perfect, if I can sleep in the same room as you,' I said serious and bashful.

'What the same room? Ben snapped. 'Sorry I can see why,'

Silence once more, I was feeling weak and tired the infection running rampart. My eyes felt heavy.

'Take forty winks if you need to,' Ben says.

'If I can, thank you,' I say resting my head back and eyes closed.

Sometime later I awoke, in hell fire pain, 'aahhhhh,' I cried.

'Emily,' Ben jumped in a panic.

'Ben I am sorry to worry you, just my neck in an awkward position,' I lie.

'Feel better for the nap,' He asks.

'How long was I asleep,' I say rubbing my neck.

'A while,' he smiles 'But you needed it,'

'Can you tell me some more of your story, no pressure though,' He asks.

Silence fell whilst I composed myself.

'Well, all sorts of things began to happen to me, my hair began to fall out, my fingers became all knotted and gnarled. My brain kept forgetting, also you can't get your words out when talking to people. I think not able to remember the basic things was hard to understand, my body hurts all over, no control over my urinal bowel. Gastro problems, swallowing and dryness of the throat became a bind. Walking was hard with my hips and back. He would keep yelling at me over and over again, 'Your broken, your nothing, no one will ever love you in this state,' Then he would hit me or punch, because I was too weak to fight his cruel words,' I say remembering the times, closing my eyes and hug myself closer and trembling.

'Emily, stop,' Ben began 'Your soul is hurting me,' he cries.

Ben looked at the road whipping a tear from his eyes, and a little sniffy act. His face was stubbly and sad.

*'Ben was beautiful when he was sad and distressed, is that wrong to think that. His face was handsome, and those lips were kissable, and to be kissed slowly and full of passion and seduction. He was loveable and he gave out a good hug. Oh! Ben you are so wonderful and loyal, I feel alive when you are near me, you make me safe and warm, you make my heart miss a beat and legs go weak. You are stuck in my head, under my skin,'* I think to myself.

'I am sorry to upset you,' was all he could say.

Silence again as we drove.

'What could I say, the worst of her pain has given the sweetest woman I have ever met since Cassie. The worst life she has endured, and no one even knew. Her life makes my life so trivial and pathetic and clueless as a doctor,' He thought as he glanced at Emily and back to the road ahead.

'Ben will you remain alone for the rest of your life, not that I am any good at this stuff myself. But would you not want to move on with your life and find out there that one person that cares for you,' I ask, looking at his stubble and kissable face. Somehow that was asked on the fact could I do it.

He turned to look at me intensely and then looked away.

'I am confused,' he thought. 'I know that a special someone is out there, and I have a lot of love, passion, tenderness, and patience I can share. Maybe walk into that person, but have I not already, her pale face with all its floors, spider veins and patches of old age creeping up. With her mousey brown hair with warm highlights with grey escaping. Is it me I have succumbed to life and feelings that she makes me feel, being alive again, my heart pounds and my pulse races when I look at her. She makes me feel good, I love her, 'What did I just say,' Ben thinks and smiling.

Ben smiled and his eyes shone an alive colour. I felt embarrassed when I saw his intense stare he was pulling as in silent mode.

*'Oh, have I done something wrong,' I thought. 'He is incredibly handsome, and he is talking with me, damn amazing. He Rescued Emily, me, of all people, he could have gone on and left me still on the Island and I would have killed myself. But him...!*

Outside the hills were rolling by and traffic no stop passing us by, I felt tired again feeling the life draining from me.

Ben watched as Emily dropped into a gentle sleep. 'She is so alone, no one cares for her or loves her. At least she could sleep next to me without worry, If I got close to her would she scream to keep away from her, being a man. Why? Has she lost the will to have a better life, what will happen. She needs to fight,' Ben thought as he glanced at her softly sleeping.

I went into a deeper sleep and found him waiting for me there, he made my body shake violently and was sick. He never said a word just told me with his face you need to be taught a lesson. Raising his hand and swung at my face with his hand fisted, then it hit me, I screamed, at the same time screamed aloud and woke with a jump. My heart beating so fast I was lightheaded.

'Emily, are you all right, your safe now, it was only a dream,' He said taking my hand and raised it to his lips and kissed my fingers, as he continued driving.

His touch calmed me, his lips were so soft, and he kissed my fingers as though they would break if it put pressure on them. I felt electricity rush through my body and things stirred that I thought were dead. My breathing slowed down to normal.

'Bad dreams,' he soft softly. 'It is only a dream, you are safe now,' He says still holding my hand.

'Sorry,' I say

Ben went sad and miserable for a few moments.

'You know when my wife died and I had to bring up my son, I felt scared and lonely. Thinking there was no one to help me with him, work and living. My parents shocked me when they said they can help, and my brother and sister were perfect. But it still became hard, the feeling of wasting their time and palming him off to others. Thinking am I bringing him up right, I continued with being a doctor, but had no one to hold me to say you are doing great and no one to love when passion struck me. I ended up thinking I was happy, but in truth I am not happy, he was bought up a good boy with the help of others.' Ben says.

'What is your doctor job, what do you specialise in,' I ask.

'I do many things, work in a hospital in the Arthritis Rheumatology department, also a GP in a practice if needed, then operations that relate to Arthritis I do. Like to talk to people as well, pick up strays that need help,' he replies.

'A multi tasked doctor, who picks up strays, have you seen a lot of dead bodies, and any have escaped death,' I ask.

'I can help you with your pain, you know,' he said quietly, remembering the day Cassie was in pain and they could not stop it.

I looked at his face, with horror and then softened to love.

'Thank you, I know,' I replied, suspicious.

*'A doctor that can help with the pain, suppose he can help me, but he will soon depart, and he will go back to being a doctor and I may well die. I need to be with him still, what am I saying being damaged is challenging work to move on and maybe find another. I need him still.'* I thought as sadness struck my heart like a knife. *'Feel strange, feel soppy things, like I was back in college and those feelings of love inside for another came pouring out. But he is only helping me and does not love me feels only pity that he gives me, because I am broken mentally and physically and pathetic. Just Pity! But I need him,'*

I bowed my head in shame and defeat.

'Was it only pity that led you to help me home, I mean is that what I will receive from my parents and my kids if they want me, will they reject me, was it just pity?' I yelled the last part.

Ben gasped and jumped a little. Silence fell again between us. Then the car stopped, and Ben got out and walked around to my side, opened the door, and helped me exit the vehicle.

'Ben?' I questioned.

He then took me in his arms and held so gently.

'Emily of course I pity you, who would not, you have had a terrible life. How can I not pity you for that, but over this short journey we have had, you have made me investigate my own life and figure out my own way. You make me feel good when you are with me and unbelievably, I am having feelings for you I can't explain, so please let me believe,' He said.

His warm breath washed over my head as he kissed it, I was shocked and could say nothing, I put my arms around him and pushed myself closer to his body.

'Now, cup of tea because I need a pee,' he says smiling embarrassed.

We made our way to the services, and he went to the men's and I ladies rest rooms. All the people in the world seems to be here, crowds are not my forte, as I need to change my dressing. When I came out, he was waiting for me, the dressing went into the sanitary bin, so no one saw it in the bin. The wound was slowing opening. I took hold of Bens Hand and huddled up to him as we walked.

'Ben, I'm scared so many people.' I said sweating a little.

He put his arm around me and pulled me close. Leading me to a small booth where we sat down.

'Strong tea,' he asks.

Then he trots off and leaves me vulnerable and open, I began to fret *'Will he find me on my own, will Ben come back or is this a chance to bail out, drive away never to be seen again, God, I am pitiful. What was I thinking, running away.' I thought.*

People all shapes and sizes walked past the booth we were in none stop almost, boyfriend, girlfriend, husband and wife, lovers, and innocent children.

'Here some tea,' Ben said sitting next to me, putting the drinks in paper cups on the table.

I grabbed his arm, 'I thought you would not come back,' I almost cried.

*'Wait, rewind, when we got out of the car, he said he had feelings for me he can't explain,'* I thought suddenly.

I looked at him, he turned to look at me, we stayed that way for a few moments. 'Thank you for the tea,' I say smiling.

Ben was not fazed by what he said in the car park, maybe I heard different.

'You forget being a GP, you hear pity all day every day, the patient thinks we show empathy out of pity especially the cancer patients. We do pity the person inside of us, but really, we see it as respect for their pain and suffering, because we couldn't in a million years know what they really go through inside of them that we can't see. So, all we can do is help them suffer less and give them the best care we can within our budgets, also with ourselves being tentative and helpful and sometimes we even shed a tear for them behind closed doors. Because patients were in my thoughts at home you can't just switch off,' Ben said with his eyes in a stare at his coffee cup.

'Ben what if you don't love yourself?' I ask quietly

'Then we must work to find that love because it is in there somewhere, in that black hole of despair that there is no escape from. Until you see it the light will only beckon you to follow it. The light that leads to hope and self-worth then you can find yourself and love, then the most important thing that hidden smile that once or twice you let slip, it radiates such love and light, it may be the end of your dark days,' He says smiling as he captures my eyes looking into his for moments of time.

I sat speechless, what a deep analogy of lives, is it possible '*I Love Him,*' for real.

'Can you help me with that?' I question

'If you let me?' he replies.

'It was not particularly bad really when he never came home from being out all day, which meant he was with her. That meant no beating for me for a bit, sometime to heal. But I was so miserable, I wanted to die, just die, could not take no more,' I said staring into his eyes.

'But look, where are you now, with me, escaping and going home,' He smiled.

I thought for a few moments and then smiled from ear to ear still looking at him. For a moment I felt good about myself, I was away from brutal harm, away in a car with a stranger and a doctor also incredibly handsome one at that, nearly home.

'Ben, I need to sleep now,' I say feeling tired and drained, as I began to close my eyes.

Ben helped me back to the car and into it and I passed out.

# Lock ness

I was still asleep when I vaguely heard the voice of Bens gentle tone.

'Emily wake up, we are here,' His voice was sweet and angelic.

Ben had let her sleep as much as he could as he drove, he enjoyed watching her face as it scrunched in pain and then relax, as if the nightmare had stopped for a moment. He kept checking to see if she was still alive every so often because her wound must be agony right now.

'Here is the end of the line, and you need help now,' he said aloud.

I opened my eyes, and the good doctor was almost nose to nose with me.

'Have I died and gone to heaven,' I asked.

'God forbid,' Ben said jumping and tearing his face away from me, I felt a little jolt to the heart, *'I could have kissed him,'* I thought.

Then my body wracked with pain, I felt the bruises and the tired bones, and my stab wound as painful as can be.

'Aaaaaaahhhhh,' I screamed 'It hurts,'

'Crap have you got tablets for it all,' he asked in a panic. Not knowing what he can do for her.

'In my bag,' I cried 'Where are we?'

'We are at Loch Ness and Mrs Macready's home by the loch,' He replied.

Ben got Emily's bag, opened it, and found said pills and a big pile of dressings, he handed her the tablets.

'What are these for? 'He thought, really, he knew the reason.

'Loch Ness really?' I said excited as I put tablets in my mouth and swallowed 'The sun is going down as well,'

I got out of the vehicle, Ben wanted to ask questions, but he waited.

'Did you say Mrs MacCready's house,' I questioned.

I looked around and the sun was low, then the Loch sat before me surrounded by trees and shrubs. It glimmered with the passing sun. It had sparkles on the small gushes of waves that rippled across the water. It was beautiful, I saw the house on the shoreline.

'It is beautiful isn't it,' Ben said standing beside me. 'It will be a perfect night to star gaze,'

'Emily, this house we are at is the home of a lady I have known for a long time, we will stay here tonight,' Ben says as he stood next to me tall and kind.

'This is kind of you both,' I smiled weakly

'Right, shall we go in,' he said beckoning for me to follow.

Ben and I walked up to the door, as it was flung open by a little lady with a greying black bun on her head. Plump wearing a knee length dress that your Great Granma would wear. The colour was beige and white, with a white pinafore over the top. She had the sweetest smile you could ever imagine.

'Hello Ben, so nice to see you again,' She said smiling in a very Scottish accent.

'Hello Maggie, this is so nice that you could put us up at short notice,' Ben replied.

'Not a problem, we love you, please come in,' she said still smiling.

'Maggie this is Emily Dawood, and I am taking her home,' He said pointing to me.

Maggie looked shocked at her appearance, feeling a great deal of pity and sorrow.

'Nice to meet you,' I say smiling.

'Ben, we only have one room left, it is a double, you ok sharing,' Maggie asked.

Ben looked horrified.

'Yes, thank you that is great, we can share,' I snapped.

'But, Emily,' Ben began.

'Ben, we are adults are not we,' I said smiling.

'Well, yes,' he replied shocked.

That was a clever idea, staying close to him was the key, share a bed together, we are not lovers but friends. The thought of being close to him made me warm and fuzzy inside. I knew the stab wound was killing me slowly, but he cares. My heart thumped and pulse raced.

*'Those days of happiness when I was once loved by a man that once love me loved back, when I was so young and then it all went wrong. The beating, the hitting, the kicking, it still hurts. The Psychological scars can never be healed, why? Did I not leave or even fight back, but here I am, escaped free, nearly home with another man that I think I have fallen in love with,'* I thought.

'Emily,' Ben says.

Ben broke my thoughts back to the now.

'Emily are you sure?' Ben questioned.

'Yes, Ben sure,' I reply.

We headed into the house, it was warm and cosy, the hallway of the house was decorated in a dirty cream colour, with a patterned Red and Black colour wall paper. To the left was the living room and right was another sitting room. The kitchen and dining room seemed to be at the back of the house. With a downstairs toilet that was on the right further along the stairs. It was rather old and stuck in an old world of sixties fashion, but it was lovely. The fire was on in the living room and the second seating area.

'Emily, are you all right,' Ben asked, he looked worried.

'Ben, I am good,' I say smiling.

The truth was I am not ok, this I think is my final stop, this is a lovely place to die a star gazing night with Ben at Loch Ness Scotland.

Maggie took us upstairs on a dusky blue carpet leading onto the landing. Leading us to a bedroom at the far end of the landing.

'Here we are,' Maggie says.

'There was a blue carpet on the floor that your feet sank into, and a large King-sized bed in blue and white. Bedside table was white on either side of the bed, chest of drawers and a wardrobe, the window looked onto the lake. The sun was nearly sunken into the lake, it was seriously beautiful, so humble to see it.

'Ok, what tablets do you want,' Ben asks.

He tipped the contents of her bag onto the bed and was looking at them.

'Pregabalin, Methotrexate, Hydroxychloroquine, co-codamol, and others,' he began as he fingered them all. 'What about these,' Holding up the wound dressings.

'Grabbed what I could,' I lied, looking away.

'Maggie will be cooking us some dinner tonight, so be ready,' Ben smiled.

Ben had laid out all my tablets, and I took them all.

'What happens when you take them, meaning any side effects,' Ben asked.

'Not sure, the doctor gave me them and never went back to any consultants until the yearly check-up,' I say. Then went quiet.

'Ok take a shower and I will find some clothes for you to change into, 'he says smiling.

*'Damn why does he smile, so, all the time? Was or is he trying to hide his anger and pity for me, I hate that everyone pities me, my own stupid fault, I got myself into this mess,'* I thought.

'Ben,' I began

'Yes,' He replied.

'Do you pity me, is that why you are helping me?' I began. Looking at the floor.

Ben was taken aback by that question, he had to think of the right words to say, they froze his heart and his brain to his lips.

I took my towel and headed for the bathroom, no words spoken, no looks of pity and help me!

# My God

L ater that evening and not many words spoken, I found myself alone in the room that we share together. Leaving the shower room and found some trousers and a t-shirt with a jumper laid on the bed for me. Ben was not in the room, and no words were spoken when he left. *'Perhaps he wanted me to have some private time. Was he still worried about feeling pity and is it at all pity. Can he find the right words, to make it better for me. I am the worst person, to drive him away. But these clothes he has acquired for me, they are so welcome, because I have nothing to wear.'* I thought.

Sighing, I touched the trousers, *'One day I will tell someone my whole life story, my feelings, my irrational thoughts of killing myself. Thoughts that were real to me and in the end my desperation led to it, no one could ever understand what domestic abuse is really like. Only those that went through it themselves would now understand me and what feelings we have. It is horrific, and pity for us to bear would be great. You can never be the person you once were. You end up struggling to keep going through life, not letting people touch you, afraid of a man touching you and afraid of yourself, and afraid of what you might do. Then to top it all off, I end up with Rheumatoid Arthritis and Fibromyalgia, then other problems arrive that you can't control, the medication for the diseases come along. I am useless to anyone, the hits and hurt are so bad they affect your bones and tissues, leaving walking difficult and day to day life is terrible sometimes, it is sole destroying.* I thought sadly. '*Then Ben came along and saved me, took my hand, and unfroze me from the spot I stood on, and led me to freedom. Pity, his eyes give it away. Looked after me, even though he knows about my knife wound. He still takes care of me, as much as he can. I should tell of my wound, but I am too proud, as it shows the moments of my weakness. But as each hour goes on, I feel weaker and sicker, why? Can't I tell him though,*' I added to my thoughts.

Lynx man's shower gel and wet washed hair, I did not flinch when Ben knocked and came in.

Ben saw Emily wrapped in a towel, frozen to the spot, 'Oh, sorry thought you would have done by now,' he began and stopped dead in his tracks, as his eyes fell upon her bruises and scars.

'Oh God!' Ben says gasping in horror as he raised his hands to his mouth.

He saw my back full of scars and bruises black and blue. There were four scars in a row on the middle of my back and shoulders. Scars of what possibly could have been a belt and were left to heal on their own, horrific bite marks that scarred.

'Emily I am sorry,' He began.

Ben then rushed over to me, and gently took me in his arms and pulled me close to him. He could smell the Lynx shower gel and her hair smelt of a tropical forest. He breathed in the scent and felt quiet a happy feeling. His fingers without thinking lightly touched her scars. I winced and put my face into his chest in shame. He ran his fingers gently across them again and it made me shiver slightly.

'Emily,' he began.

I could feel his warm breath on my skin, it was quiet satisfying.

'Ben, I can't talk to you, yet please I am so ashamed,' I pleaded, leaving my face on his chest.

He kept hold of me gently. 'Emily that is all right, but one day,' He began.

'Ben's heart cracked but felt her warmth flick through him like a bolt of lightning, or a light switch on his sole. The feeling was overwhelming him. It was in his chest and spread filling his body like water running through his veins. The last time he felt like this was at eighteen and Cassie. The feeling of love all over again. But! Was it pity, love, do I Love her? But he felt love, his heart thumping and butterflies flipping in his tummy.

'Thank you, Ben,' I say still in his chest.

'Now, I will have a shower and you put some clothes on and keep warm, ok,' Ben said gently. He kissed the top of my head.

'Ok,' I say ashamed.

'*I let him touch me, and half naked as well. He saw my scars and my bruises on the visible parts at this time,*' I thought ashamed.

Ben went into the bathroom, and I began to change into the long trousers and top, with the jumper. I looked like a vagabond with scatty hair. 'But I am free,' I say quietly to myself.

Ben came out of the bathroom with a towel wrapped around his waist, the body of a god on show. Every ripple on his tummy and black greying hair on his chest, tanned skin, and fit legs.

I turned around so he could dress.

'Ben,' I ask

'Yes Emily,' Ben replied.

'We have been very adult about sharing haven't we, and the funny thing is I may feel ashamed that you saw me, I don't feel bad about myself, because if nothing else, you saved me. I will never forget that ever, thank you Ben,' I said feeling good.'

'Very adult I feel ashamed as a man, that your sacred womanly body has been defiled by another man that you trusted, a monster. You suffered torture, but you trusted me to be able to touch you and see some of you that has been hurting. You make me feel confused and scattered. Feelings that are odd, I feel that you would let me see, the fact that I let you see me like this, just feels good,' Ben admitted.

'For me is it because you are a doctor, I don't know,' I say sadly.

Ben took me in his arms from behind me, I stood tall and accepted it, for now his arms felt safe and calm.

Ben held Emily and he felt his heart sinking into his stomach, all her pain and torture is an exceptional case of domestic abuse. But this was a start of a new man with a new goal.

'Ben, things behind closed doors stay that way until the breakout that must find a way to cope with being free. That is the hardest part, your spirit is broken, and the only thing left is to take it, then the despair sets in.' I cry.

We stood together for a long time, and he kissed the top of my head.

'You need warm food, dinner is ready,' He says.

# Dinner

Ben and I headed downstairs, both of us quiet, I was thinking of the nice moment when Ben was holding me and touching my scars and the way he smelt.

The Dining room had one large dining table and eight chairs, there was a dresser in solid pine with plates, saucers and cups with the Loch and the Loch Ness Monster on it. The display was rather nice. Then a log fireplace with a small fire burning. There was another small dining table for two in the corner by a small window, the floor was in wooden pine. The room a classic cream colour. The walls were dotted here and there with paintings of Loch Ness, a castle sprung up in a few paintings. Green curtains with that cosy feel.

'This is a quaint nice house, so peaceful,' I commented.

'Thank you dear,' Mrs MacCready said as she stood behind us.

'Maggie, thank you,' Ben said smiling as he turned to face her.

'Hello again dear, I think you can sit and have some dinner,' she said guiding us to the small table with two chairs.

We sat opposite each other.

'Ben,' I say looking down at the table.

'Emily,' he replies.

'Errum ......,' I began then unable to speak. 'Nothing,'

Then Mrs MacCready bought the dinner out, it was venison, Roast Potatoes, and a selection of Vegetables.

'Is this all for me?' I asked shocked.

'Yes dear, all for you,' she replied, shocked at the question.

'You don't have to eat it all,' Ben replied.

'This is like a dream,' I began 'to think I was given a kind moment by you, Doctor Ben Hardy, and here I am by the Lake of Loch Ness and freedom,' I say quietly.

'Emily,' He began.

'Yes,'

'You look very pale and peaky, are you all right,' He asked.

'Could not be better,' I replied lying

The dinner was eaten, as much as possible, and a glass of wine was drunk slowly.

'A toast, Emily, to freedom,' Ben held up his glass toward her.

I picked up my glass and we both clinked our glasses together and sipped.

'Thank you,' I smile.

'Pleasure is all mine,' He replies.

Ben looked into her eyes, could see slowly the life force leaving her, her peaky white face, with no rosy cheeks that made his heart ache and bought slight tears to his eyes.

Dinner ended, and it was delicious, the fire was warm and cosy, we both left the table and sat on the sofa. I sat straight and Ben relaxed backwards.

'Ben on my back those scars you saw,' I began. 'They hurt me bad the belt was leather and hard,'

'Emily, you don't have to continue,' Ben snapped concerned.

'Ben, I need to, they are from his leather belt, that he repeated time and time again over the same wounds, it never seemed to heal, but it has now. This would be a passion killer, as they say,' I say looking into his eyes. 'It was easy for him, because it, was my back and always had clothes on,' I added. 'These were my dark days,' My tears that I shed were like a river. These were the days when I could not move, then slept on the floor where I fell,'

'You have been very brave, you endeared that and still lived to see another beating,' Ben sadly said.

'I had a mindset of one day someone would be kind and rescue me,' I said 'I can say that it happened you Rescued Me,' I smiled.

'Tell me about your children, do you know where they are now?' He asked.

I thought a moment.

'My children, left with my mother and father, when they were ten and twelve, just to keep them safe. They met me at the port and returned on the ferry with them. Then I heard nothing from them again. Tore my heart apart, never stopped thinking about them day to day always in my mind. Don't know where they are now, know nothing about them, but I want to see them again. My parents stopped calling and never heard from them again. I want to see them, but will they want to see me,' I said.

I sipped my wine; it was a Rose Wine and tasted sweet.

'Emily, things may be all right, you need to take it one step at a time,' Ben said putting his hand on mine.

His touch sparked electric shocks through my system, my heart thumped, and that wonderful feeling of being alive. I am not a teenager.

But the perfect situation will soon end abruptly.

> I had a few moments when my diseases
> gave me peace, ready to give up, but
> him, a kind and gentle soul Rescued
> Emily and now I want to live.

# Stars

**M**rs MacCready came in carrying two warm thick coats. Ben's own coat and a warm coat for me.

'Thank you, Maggie that is great,' Ben smiled as he took both the coats off her.

'No problem lovely, and enjoy your star gazing, good clear night for it,' She replies with a huge smile.

'The Stars await you,' Ben smiled.

He handed me the coat and I put it on.

Leaving the house, we went outside; it was cold and dark now. The Loch was enshrouded in a blanket of mist that clawed its way over the water toward them.

'This is so beautiful,' I say gasping.

'Isn't it,' Ben replied softly.

There were blankets lying on the floor for us, with a pile of wood with blankets laid over them as you can sit against them.

'Wow, for us,' I say my face turned to so much happiness.

'Emily, do you mind if I hold you, in a sitting lying down position against the wood, the best way to see the stars,' Ben asks.

'Not a problem,' I reply.

By this time, I could feel my life force fading away, in Ben's arms, the sky was full of stars in the sky, but the moon was only three quarters full.

'Ben, the sky is beautiful, millions of them shinning just for me, the sky at night is wonderful,' I say.

I felt weak and coughed a little and shivered. 'I love it, the sky at night, so wonderful, 'I whisper,

'Emily,' Ben began

'Ben,'

'I phoned an ambulance. I saw the dressing in the bathroom, so much blood, you are looking white, and your eyes are losing the shine,' He says 'I don't want you to die,' Ben cries.

'He would give me every day, a list of things he wanted me to do, and what he wanted me to do for dinner every day, for just him and not me. I left had to do them or I would not be allowed to be fed or watered just like a dog. When things were rough, I took It, but before I left I snaped and took hold of a knife and threatened to kill him, but I was so weak that he overpowered me and then stabbed me in my left side instead. I glued it together and using the dressings to keep me going. Making it to freedom,' I said as tears rolled down my face.

'But, thank you Ben, you helped me to just do that, But I am sorry, Ben my life force is crying for help,' I say weakly.

'Emily why not tell me?' Ben replies.

'Because, this has been amazing, my Angel saved me, showing me kindness and pity. That took me on an amazing journey.' I say

'Emily you need to stay awake. Ok, for just a bit longer, please,' he begged.

'Thank you,' I say again.

I moved my head to come face to face with him and smiled, not knowing what he was doing and hearing the ambulance sirens, outside almost. He bent his head further, so his lips touched mine and he kissed, and I kissed him back, he was soft and gentle, although mine were cold he tasked of love, and I wanted more. The first loving kiss in an exceptionally long time and perfectly sweet.

That was my last moment awake before my eyes closed into the blackness I went as it unfolded before me like a blanket, my body relaxed almost limp.

'Emily, Emily, no wake up,' Ben cried in grief.

I was in darkness, just standing there in the cold, there was a distant light. A faint light though.

'Where am I,' I said as my voice echoed around me.

It was cold, as I stood shivering.

'It's cold, where am I? Ben where are you? I'm scared,' I cried hugging myself.

Searching around in the darkness only led to more darkness, my footsteps were the only sounds I could make out although I had no shoes on, and the floor was solid and cold.

Voices I could hear voices.

'This way quick,' a male voice said loudly. It echoed all around me.

Voices, walk toward the light, keep going Emily. Walk one foot in front of the other, the light was getting brighter.

# Hospital

I had managed to walk into the light, it was so bright that it hurt my eyes.

'Is this the end, the road to heaven,' I ask aloud.

It felt calm and all the heaviness had left my body and was replaced by light, weightless and calmed sole.

'Doctor Hardy,' came a male voice into my light space and echoing around me.

**'Ben, is that you, are you there,'** I thought, looking around my light,

'Dr Pardy,' Ben began 'What is the verdict,'

'Well she will live, but for a while it was touch and go. Ben her injuries are horrific all over her body, what happened to her,' Dr Pardy said in horror.

'As you know of her diseases, the rest is from years of Domestic Abuse, a lot of it,' He replies sick to his stomach.

'The husband was a very cruel man, but at least she can heal. You will have my report later, she is being closed then will go to the recovery room.' Dr Pardy says,

*'Why can't I open my eyes; the bright light has gone leaving me in the dark again. I want to see Ben, Ben, I love you,'* I think inside.

Close my eyes and sleep a while.

I had a wonderful site in my dreams today, my mum and dad were next to me.

'Hello, Darling,' she says.

I could not see them but could feel her hand in mine her touch was so warm and caring.

'Please be well, everyone is waiting for you, I have bought your favourite flowers assorted colour Gerberas,' She is saying crying now.

*'Why are you crying, please don't cry mum,'* I say sadly inside my head.

'Hello sweetie, it's dad, I'm sorry,' He was crying like a baby now as he held my hand.

*'No, I'm sorry, for everything, thank you for coming to me,'* I cried inside.

Tears ran down my face on the outside.

'Granma,' said another voice.

'Mum it's Toni and James and not forgetting grandad,' Toni my daughter says.

*'My parents, my children, they all have come to see me. That makes my heart feel happy, I feel happy,'* I say crying in my dream.

There was light across my eyes.

'Emily, it is time to wake up now. You need to come back to me, I miss you and I love you,' Ben says as he stroked my face then brushed my lips with his.

I followed the sound of his voice and into the light, into reality.

'Ben, is that you,' I said in a whisper.

My eyes opened slowly onto Ben's beautiful eyes.

'Emily,' He said with such joy taking my hand and kissing then to hold it.

'Am I alive, Ben, did I die, and this is paradise,' I whispered.

'No dummy, you are very much alive, I thought you would never wake up and come back to me,' He says smiling.

My eyes adjusted, as Ben put his face close to mine, it made my heart race, and I blushed a lot.

'How are you feeling? Sick, tired, pain anywhere?' Ben asked concerned then he pulled his face away.

'Kiss me again,' I just said. 'kiss me,'

So, he leant forward and did so, my right hand came up to touch his face as he did so, soft, but enthusiastic. He moved off my lips.

'Thank you, Now I know I am alive,' I say smiling.

I moved a little, my left side was in pain and my hand had swollen due to the canula in it.

'How long have I been asleep?' I asked

'Three weeks and two days,' Ben replied, 'they were the worst weeks of my life since Cassie,' Ben sighs.

Then I start to cry.

'Emily, what is it?' Ben asked taking my hand again

'I'm sorry to have worried you so much, in my dreams I saw or rather felt my mum and dad and my children, grandma and grandad, they came to see me after all these years.' I cried 'I could feel them but then they were gone, they were gone. I felt you close by all the time, even held my hand, you love me, even though the state of me is disgusting and dirty. My body defiled and broken, yet you love me,' I cried.

'Hey you will pop your stitches,' He said smiling, lifting himself from the armchair he sat in and holding my hand, then he stroked my face.

It was such a lovely feeling as tingles went down my spine.

'My side hurts and my hair must be a mess,' I said yawning 'Ben you should go home to Axminister we are so far away; I will be all right,' I say.

'Little lady, we are already in Axminster Hospital, and I work here. You were transferred after your operation,' He replied.

'What? Really?' I gasped, closing my eyes thank full and happy. 'Ben my head feels woozy and dizzy,' I was closing my eyes to sleep, 'Thank you, I love you,' I sleepily say then I was asleep.

My dreams were of Ben kissing me, and my family that I missed so dearly.

The next day around lunch time I awoke. To see an older lady sitting in the armchair knitting.

'Hello,' I say smiling 'are you a ghost,'

'Hello honey,' she said smiling and putting the knitting down.

'Mum,' I asked, coming around properly, she was much older than me, black greying hair a wrinkled stained face. A slim build and a happy face, I smiled with tears in my eyes.

'Mum,' I cried. 'I'm sorry for every thing,' I say.

'At least you remember me,' She said smiling she stood up and kissed my cheek.

I was happy she was here because she sees me, she did not have to come. I left and endured, cut them off, sent my children to live with them, with nothing. I burst out in tears. She sat on the bed, bent over me, and held me to her.

'I am so grateful your safe and alive, I worried over and over the years for your safe return, I love you so much,' she says crying.

She said that to me, the one that let her down, Me!

'Mum,' came another female voice.

Mum pulled away to reveal a man and a woman.

'Toni and James, oh my, I have missed you so much,' I say shocked.

I was worried they would reject me and say harsh words that I deserve but do not want to hear.

Toni was small in height like me, long beautiful mousey brown hair. Slim with healthy skin, her eyes were showing such emotion. James was slim wearing a light grey suit, black swept back hair and very handsome.

They both ran to me and hugged me, one on either side, crying real tears, me saying 'I am sorry and so glad you are here,' I cry with them.

In came dad. And he hugged me.

This is an amazing day, and I will never forget it, ever. Toni had become a lawyer and at thirty-two she was single. James was twenty-nine and a lawyer in domestic abuse cases to men and women. Not married either.

They were talking all together with me in the middle listening and incredibly happy. I drifted off to sleep.

Later I awoke again, Ben was sitting next to me reading. But I was not in the hospital room, I was in a room with other people wearing face masks and not moving. It was a peaceful moment but had a scary reality for it was a place of death I could smell it, halfway between the living and the dead. Was this my end, those people are frozen on the between worlds not knowing which way to go. My mask was giving me oxygen as my chest was feeling heavy and I felt odd, I needed to cough I mean really cough, so I naturally coughed moving the mask.

Ben took my hand, then took my mask away and produced water for me to drink.

'Welcome back,' he said softly.

'Ben am I alive,' I ask drinking the water. 'is this real,'

'Intensive care you had a mishap and needed extra care,' he replied 'you manged to get a little infection which put you in danger. But you are awake, so it looks good,'

I spent a few more days in Intensive care, then moved back to my room where worried faces waited.

'Good Morning,' Ben said smiling.

'Morning,' I replied happy.

'Emily I need to talk to you,' He said in a deep voice and heavy hearted.

'Ok,' I say worried.

Here it comes the talk on glad I am ok and found my family that has excepted me. He must move on and so do I, I saved, no, I Rescued Emily, that I will never forget.

'Ben, I know you must go now, you Rescued Emily and I am so grateful, thank you so much, I will never forget you. You will always be in my heart,' I say sadly.

Ben looked shocked at me.

'Emily, I Love you,' He said.

'What?' I say shocked.

'I love you so much, it makes my heart ache,' He said.

He bent down and kissed me softly and I retuned his kiss and tasted his tongue as he played with mine. He tasted sweet, putting my hand on his cheek, he put his hand on mine.

'I love you,' I say as we just kissed.

He sat on the bed and took me in his arms, I love him my saviour my everything.

# Dead

I was feeling good, he loves me and I him. I like how he holds me so that I won't hurt. I was told by him that I would be in hospital for some time, as I was so thin, they had to get me back to a healthy look.

Ben came every day, sometimes we kissed and sometimes he would just hold me, and other times talk about his day.

'Emily, I have seen your whole body from tip of your head to the tips of your toes, I have seen the scars the bruises and the violations. My love is not pity; my love is because you are an interesting soul. The way you smile slightly how the right side of your mouth turns up. The way you show genuine happiness and gratitude, your lips are so kissable and you feel right when I hold you. How you broke down my walls just slowly making me feel human again. I Love you for you,' he said kissing me.

'As you have seen, does it not repulse you, when naked we touch and hold, does it not repulse you, making sweet love to me,' I say with tears in my eyes.

'Emily, I just see you,' He replies kissing me again.

I was worried about myself and about my body. But my mum and dad visited almost every day, and Toni and James would follow when they could.

James came to visit one evening. He was handsome in his blue suit, twenty-nine and not married. But still lived with mum and dad.

'Mum, they showed us your injuries,' He began eyes darted to the floor.

I gasped in horror.

'What?' I said shocked.

'Now, I know why you sent us away to live with grandma and grandad,' he replied.

'James, you had to go. He was beginning to turn to you both,' I replied, 'My children had to be safe,' I filled up with tears.

He hugged me and said, 'I love you, mum. Thank you, for saving us, I will never forget the day when my mum Emily got rescued.'

I hugged him and he kissed my cheek. 'I love you, thank you for not forsaking me,'

We held each other.

'Hey you, hot shot criminal lawyer of domestic abuse, you did good,' I said smiling.

I was on my own again.

In the end I had to have physio slowly and had my meals monitored and the drips would be sending nutrition in. So, I was in there for almost two months healing, growing muscles learning the art of eating three meals a day, Ben worked there so he visited me every day.

One evening I had gone to the bathroom and on the way out, by the door to the room, stood Dale smirking at me. Waiting for me, to take me back with him.

I gasped in horror holding my chest, my heart raced and pulse quickened I could hear my heart beating so loud. My head exploded in fear. Then I passed out into darkness.

A bit later Ben walks in, and there I was on the floor.

'Emily, oh my god,' he said panicking. He pressed the distress bell and lifted me onto the bed. I was breathing but my pulse raced.

Head bleeding, from hitting the floor. Nurses cleaned my head and doctors did their checks and wired me back up to the machines. Ben, he sat next to me stocking my hair, and cheek, he was holding my hand. I woke up and squeezed his hand.

'Emily' he said sitting up.

'Ben, what happened,' I asked. My head hurt and I felt sick.

'Not sure, but hopefully, you can fill us in on that,' He said begging.

'I came out of the bathroom, and over at the door stood Dale, laughing, and looking at me with killer eyes.' I tell him.

He took me in his arms, I froze up and passed out. My body was screaming with agony, the hitting and I grew hot and the punching and kicking came back. My chest feels tight, I grew hot and sweaty. Grabbing my clothes, I began to become breathless.

'Emily, are you all right,' Ben asked worried.

I heard Ben's voice and that bought me back to reality.

'I came from the bathroom and looked up. There stood in the doorway laughing, smiling to take me back was Dale,' I said.

My pain came back in my side then my head hurt I must have banged it on the floor, hence the headache.

Ben held me tighter, 'Emily your safe now,' Ben sad softly.

The pain in my heart eased.

'You have been out a while, we were worried, didn't know if you would come back to me,' Ben softly says in my hair.

His embrace slackened, looking at the drips and back at me. 'Emily, we have had a journey, have we not. I rescued you, yes, but you have rescued me also. I have never wanted a relationship because of Cassie, told myself to never love again, but you made me feel alive, with the confessions and touching that we did for each other, made my heart drop the chains and wanting to love again. The passion in my heart, which makes my loin cloth move.' He giggled. 'I want you, and no one else can have you. I got to the point of loving you, I am in love with you, but I am scared you do not love me back. You may not need a man after all they do to you, and I understand that.' he added

I thought for a moment at to what he said.

'Ben. You are in love with me, thank you, because I am in love with you. Ben, you rescued Emily, with our time together on that short journey, you were kind to me. Pity for me can turn into a false love for me, Pity, you are a kind soul. You touch me and I feel alive, grew into a woman falling in love with you, hoping we could become lovers. But you know we need to take it slow, because I want to feel all of you.' I cried sincere.

'Emily, you don't have to be afraid of me, I want to take the steps of your life with you slowly as not to hurt you. First, we need to get you healthy and home. Take each step as it comes, can I kiss you,' He asked me, and something moved for me.

'Kiss me Ben, kiss me,' I ask with vigour.

He touched my lips with his, cupped my face. Softly he parted my lips and played with my tongue, I played with Bens as our kiss went deeper, my body exploded into happiness, something moved in my loin cloth area. Pulling him into me, I wanted to feel all of him against me.

'Erm excuse me,' came a male voice.

We broke apart feeling embarrassed. We looked at two Police Officers. The male was about six foot and a stocky build, black hair and handsome, the woman was five-foot seven I think cute to the eye.

'Hello officers can I help you,' Ben asks.

'Could we have a word doctor outside,' The male police officer asks. Ben left with them.

'We are looking for Miss Emily Dawood,' he said in his authoritative voice.

'That is whom I was with,' he replied.

'We have some sad news; Mr Dale Macdonald has been killed in an accident on the A1 and his passenger a woman we do not know has also died.' The Police Officer says sadly.

'Come in,' Ben says.

Ben sat on the bed and took my hand.

'Emily Dawood, there has been a tragic accident, a Mister Dale McDonald has been killed in a car crash on the A1 along with a woman,' He says.,

'We believe he was coming to see you, we are deeply sorry,' The female says.

'He died, he died,' I begin to laugh 'Gone died,' I laughed so hard I ended up crying.

'We can provide any bereavement counselling for you,' the woman officer says.

'Thank you, no, we have each other.' I say smiling at Ben. The police persons left.

He was gone, dead, my life could continue with no problems. Just look forward to all good things. I fear the future, but I have someone to love, and he loves me back, when I am healed, but still have the life diseases will not be easy, but with loving people by me will help me heal quicker.

# Life

I left the hospital two months later; my parents wanted me to come home, so I did. They gave me a bedroom on the ground floor as I was not walking as I should yet, the physio helped me in the hospital, I was at the weight of a healthy woman, Ben helped me with the nightmares when he stayed over with me, our nights were filled with kissing and holding each other.

My children showed me their homes and their life, learning all the time.

Ben came a lot siting and talking, and to my parents, we would go to dinner talk about everything we could, laugh and cry, each wanting more.

From it all My back and lower hips made me have dizzy spells and hardly walk a distance, but this is Life after Death and it was a wonderful feeling, thank goodness my parents loved me, and my children came back to me. I am lucky, and will cherish every moment of it, and be thank full to be alive.

Don't get me wrong, not everyone's dreams and escapes are the same as this one, it takes time to be loving someone straight away, because if you have been abused by the man you love, you can't trust men ever again. Repulsed if they come near you, dare touch you, make you feel sick and heavy, living with the nightmares of times past and the hope of how you can proceed to future life.

Don't give up, keep fighting for what is good for you and your body, and for you to believe in. It can only get better if you, manage your diseases because you are the only one that knows what hurts and what will help.

My life is much better, so can yours with some will power, just like people power…

www.ingramcontent.com/pod-product-compliance
Lightning Source LLC
Chambersburg PA
CBHW031226120626
46545CB00003B/1007